W0016692

EMERGENCY SPELLS

MAGIC
for
DIFFICULT
TIMES

◆

GAIA ELLIOT

Hardie Grant
BOOKS

PART I

✦

PART II

✦

Emergency spells for…

PART

·I·

Introduction

*'If this be magic, let it be an art
Lawful as eating.'*

Shakespeare, *The Winter's Tale*

Your connection to the earth and all life on it is both physical and spiritual, and in the casting of spells, the two meet and connect you with the universe and its innate power to nourish, support and protect. Knowing this and knowing how to use its metaphorical magic is an art that anyone can learn, through the use of spells geared towards utilising the positive energies of the universe and its four elements: earth, wind, air and fire. No spell in this book is designed to work negatively.

Throughout history and in different cultures, people have sought to use spells to focus their intuition and personal energy to effect positive change. These energies are often used symbolically through a range of representative items: herbs, candles, essential oils, coloured cloths or threads, fire and water; all can be imbued with the universe's power.

6

If you are to become a serious practitioner, it's good to have a collection of spells that is unique to you and that becomes more powerful as you develop your skills.

A spell is a mini-ritual, a way to harness and focus divine energy on an outcome you desire, either for yourself or others. You can use spells to effect positive change for others that you love and care about, as much as for yourself – for example, if they are unwell or you want to protect them in some way. You can use spells to help address intensely emotional issues, like a yearning for love or its fulfilment, to protect or safeguard someone, or even something like celebrating a new home or practising gratitude.

Spells often include incantations – words repeated to indicate an intention to the universe. These incantations are written down, kept, buried or burnt, depending on the spell. Words matter and once uttered or written down have a greater power than if left unsaid.

When it comes to casting spells, your intentions need to be positive. It goes against the universe to harbour ill will or to actively seek to promote negativity. There has to be an honest intent for improvement or peaceful resolution. You can't, for example, cast a spell on those you dislike and make bad things happen to them. Indeed, any attempt to manipulate a spell negatively can backfire on you, so it's important to remember this.

7

Believing in the power of the spells you cast doesn't always come easily to everyone. It's important to believe in your ability to take the ritual and incantations of the spells suggested and make them your own. Confidence in this comes from repetition and your own intuitive development that will occur over time and with practice. So practise your spells, it is an art that can be developed and is accessible to everyone.

Visualisation can help with casting spells too. Often we want someone else to be the focus of our spell, so it's important to be able to imagine them, and in a particular circumstance. For example, visualising the person you wish to love you holding out their hand or, if someone is sick, picturing them managing their illness in a way that works for them. Visualisation doesn't come easily to everyone either, so be sure to practise this and make it part of your spell-casting.

Time can be relevant to some spells – for example, midnight is often considered a magic time as the passage of day to night brings its own energy. Or dawn or dusk, depending on whether you want to power something up or reduce its impact.

Points of the Compass

The four points of the compass relate to the four elements of the universe and bring their own power, identifying these can be helpful when you position yourself to cast a spell.

North

Represents the element of Earth and helps ground and secure energy.

West

Represents the element of Water and is a cleansing, restorative energy.

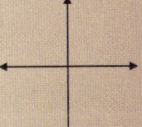

East

Represents the element of Air, and new energy, dawns and beginnings.

South

Represents the element of Fire and will help ignite a spell's energy.

9

Days of the Week

The days of the week have their own power,
given by the planets that rule them. This can
also be used to your advantage.

SUNDAY

☉

Ruled by the Sun,
literally life-giving
and strengthening.

MONDAY

☿

Ruled by the Moon,
emotionally sustaining
and peaceful.

TUESDAY

☾

Ruled by Mars,
providing masculine
power and force.

WEDNESDAY

♃

Ruled by Mercury,
enhancing communication
and connection.

THURSDAY

♂

Ruled by Jupiter,
benevolent and
kind, often lucky.

FRIDAY

♀

Ruled by Venus, planet
of beauty and love,
connects to the heart.

SATURDAY

♄

Ruled by Saturn, planet of wisdom and lessons learned.

10

Phases of the Moon

The phases of the moon can help you too, as the moon moves from new to old, waxing and waning through the course of its cycle. A new moon has a new energy and through its waxing cycle will gain strength and then, during its waning cycle it consolidates this until its culmination in a full moon, the peak of its abundance.

In addition, the moon moves through the twelve zodiac signs during the course of a month, once every two-and-a-half days, bringing the additional power of their astrological characteristics to its reflected light. The more knowledge you have of the universe in which you are casting your spell, the more you can use it to work to your advantage.

11

Tools
for Spells

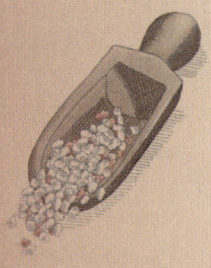

Each spell in this book references items
of intrinsic relevance to the spell, many
of which are easily found among household
items or sourced from cooking staples,
dried or growing herbs. Some you may wish
to acquire or purchase – essential oils
or crystals, for example, or your birthstone
– so that you can have them ready and
available to use. It's also useful to understand
their representative value and how this
might work to enhance the creation
of a spell and its outcome.

SALT
Use either sea salt
or Himalayan salt,
which are complete
and energised.

PINS
Either plain or topped
with coloured glass,
these help spells
to connect or pierce.

SUGAR OR HONEY
Can sweeten a spell
and the situation.

EARTH
A pinch of soil can help
ground a spell.

CAYENNE PEPPER
Contributes strong
energy that can
speed up a process.

FEATHER
Find and keep a selection
of white, brown and
coloured feathers.

GARLIC
Potent and protective,
guards against
toxic energy.

KEY
Use a key that actually
works so you know
it has the capacity
to work in a spell.

WATER
Collect rainwater
in either a glass or
ceramic container.

GOLD
This can be a piece
of jewellery, a ring
for example, that
is of value to you.

13

SILVER
Again, a piece of jewellery will serve for this.

CANDLES
Representative of the flame of life, they work to illuminate a spell and different colours have different powers.

CERAMIC CONTAINER
Never use plastic, instead use a ceramic container special to you.

GLASS CONTAINER
Sometimes transparency is part of the spell; if so, use glass. A clean jar will do.

THREADS
Different colours have different powers.

BELLS
A small bell can be used in banishment spells.

DIFFERENT COLOURED PENS AND PAPER
Writing an intention is sometimes part of the spell. Even if the paper is burnt or buried afterwards, always use ink as it is more permanent than pencil.

COMPASS
Sometimes it's useful to know which direction to face when casting a spell.

14

Magic
Numbers

8   7   *1*
   3   6
5   **2**   4

The number three has potency, as do multiples of three, while the number seven also has its own power. Your personal numerology, based on your birth date, will also have significance. For example, if your birth date is 14th April 2003, then this becomes 1+4+0+4+2+0+0+3 = 14 and then this breaks down further to 1+4 which gives you a numerology of 5. So, if this was you, the number five would be significant.

15

Herbs & Plants

Their energy is either new if fresh or more intense if dried, so you can regulate their power in a spell.

SAGE

Imparts its own wisdom, cleanses energy and helps us to focus on what really matters or how to solve a particular problem.

CLOVES

Pungent and spiky, they have the power to kill free radicals and bacteria and are anti-inflammatory.

CHAMOMILE

While it is renowned for its sedative effects, chamomile can also help us see a situation more clearly, either literally or metaphorically.

SEEDS

Collect seeds from your favourite flower or even culinary poppy seeds will do.

16

LAVENDER

Works to both calm and stimulate, depending on how it's utilised, and often works synergistically in spells to enhance other elements.

LEMON BALM

Helps to reduce both physical and emotional inflammation, so can calm the body as much as the mind.

ROSEMARY

For remembrance and to sharpen memories.

BAY

Fresh, dried, crushed or burnt, bay is the herb of victory and peace and has its place in a lot of cultures and folk remedies.

DAISY

The common daisy or *bellis perennis* has healing and reinvigorating powers, especially for the heart: pick when fresh in season and dry the flowers to use all year round.

NETTLES

Considered by many to be a weed, nettles have the power to galvanise and sting any intention into action: pick fresh or keep a stock of dried.

17

Essential Oils

Although these are not critical to all spells, they can be useful to increase their power and help your focus when spell-making.

LAVENDER
A useful alternative to fresh or dried, can help focus spells.

VETIVER
Cleansing and stimulating, this can also help clarification spells.

ROSE
Links to matters of the heart; again, you can also use fresh or dried rose petals.

YLANG-YLANG
Sweetly persuasive, connects the body and mind to enhance a spell.

BERGAMOT
A reviving oil that can strengthen and resolve intentions.

NEROLI
Cleansing and restorative, also citrusy and stimulates any spell's effect.

ROSEMARY
For remembrance, this can also lift the spirits and enhance a spell.

18

Crystals

You can choose your own favourite crystal
for the energy that resonates with your own,
but these can be useful allies in casting
an emergency spell.

QUARTZ
Regulates the power
of a spell and brings
clarity.

AMETHYST
Protective and healing
on both a physical and
emotional level.

ROSE QUARTZ
A very feminine and
loving energy, also
rebalances trust.

YOUR BIRTHSTONE
This helps focus the
energy of the universe
on you and you alone.

19

Silk or
Cotton Squares

These need only be small, and can even
be sourced from snippets of your favourite
garments, but it's important that the fabrics
are natural, so silk or cotton are best. You can
use different coloured threads too, and here
you can also include wool.

Colours

When it comes to colours, or tones of colour, whether this is ink, thread, cloth, candle wax or anything else, each will impart its own vibrational energy which you can utilise to enhance or, literally, colour the intention of your spell.

RED
Strong, male or
sexual energy.

YELLOW
Restorative,
spirit-lifting energy.

GREEN
New life and
life-affirming energy.

WHITE
Purifying,
new start energy.

BLUE
Calming,
fluid energy.

GOLD
Wealth and success
(not just material) energy.

PINK
Feminine,
healing energy.

SILVER
Creative,
fertile energy.

21

PART

· II ·

The Spells

The following emergency spells are there for just that, emergencies. But they will also work well when you need to refocus or rebalance your energies on other occasions. Remember, everyone reacts and responds to magic slightly differently and as you become more familiar with each spell, you will come to learn which chime most effectively with your individual energy at any given time. Our energy is never static but a fluid, evolving thing that we can enhance or focus through our intentions.

Working with this knowledge, grounded in the natural world, is a holistic way of living your life and will connect you with the universe to your daily advantage. Knowing what to do to restore your connection to the universe in an emergency is key and you will soon learn what components of a spell work best for you, so it may be a good idea to keep a notebook, recording the details of what you've used and how it worked out for you. Remember to date it too, as that can be helpful when trying to recall the success of a spell and the time it may have taken to be effective.

◆

Emergency Spells for Every Day

◆

During the course of a day, our energy can fluctuate, affected by both our mental or physical wellbeing. Knowing how to boost or calm this energy can be useful in an emergency and helps us get through our day, making the most of what it has to offer.

· 1 ·

TO KICKSTART YOUR DAY

YOU WILL NEED
a key, a ceramic container, cayenne pepper

1

Take a key and place it
in a ceramic container.

2

Sprinkle a little cayenne pepper
over the key.

3

Cup the container in both hands and
hold it at the level of your eyes.

4

Say aloud the incantation,
'I embrace the day and all it holds'
three times.

5

Place the container nearby and
leave it there for the rest of the day.

29

· 2 ·

IF YOU HAVE TO DO SOMETHING AT WORK FOR THE FIRST TIME AND FEEL NERVOUS

YOU WILL NEED
3 green threads, a feather, salt

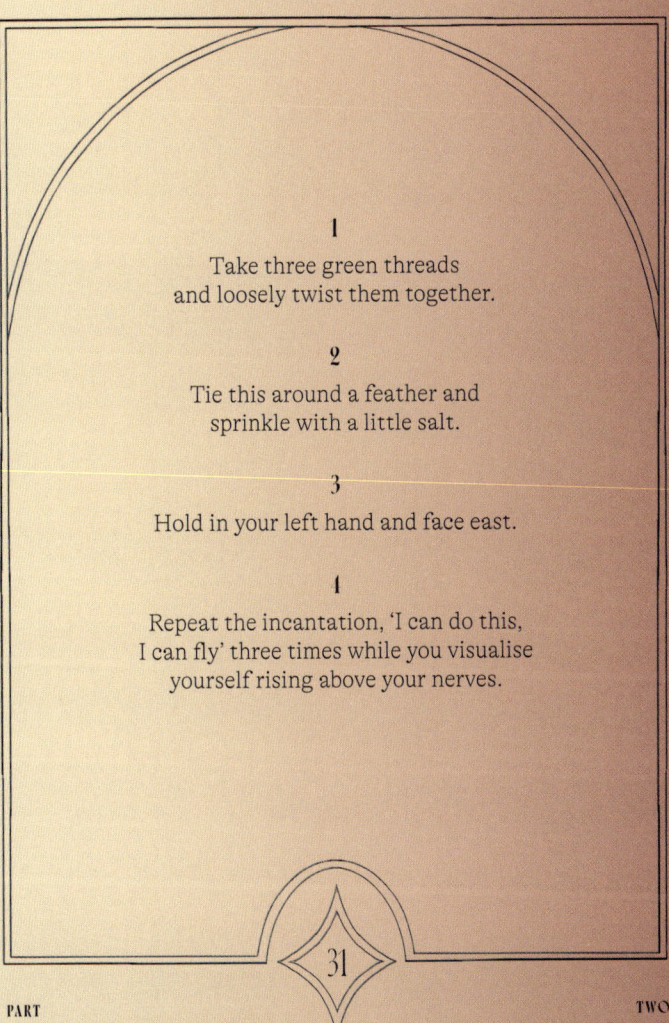

1

Take three green threads
and loosely twist them together.

2

Tie this around a feather and
sprinkle with a little salt.

3

Hold in your left hand and face east.

4

Repeat the incantation, 'I can do this,
I can fly' three times while you visualise
yourself rising above your nerves.

31

· 3 ·

TO POWER UP
DURING THE DAY

YOU WILL NEED
1 stinging nettle (fresh or dried),
a glass container or jar, bergamot oil

1

Take a fresh or dried stinging nettle,
being mindful to protect your skin.

2

Carefully place in a glass container.

3

Add a drop of bergamot oil.

4

Repeat to yourself the incantation,
'Power up, power up, power up' three times.

5

Focus on breathing deeply in between
each repetition.

· 4 ·

TO KEEP CALM AND REDUCE STRESS

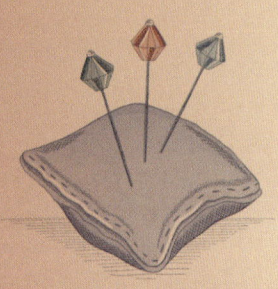

YOU WILL NEED
1 or 2 chamomile heads, 1 or 2 pins, a pink cloth

1

Take a camomile head or two and pin them
to a pink cloth to secure your intention.

2

Place in some natural light and
focus on your breath.

3

Breathe in for four counts, hold for two
and out through the nose for four counts.

4

Repeat, 'I am calm, I am at peace,
I am calm' three times.

5

Then sit quietly for a few minutes
before continuing with your day.

TO PRACTISE GRATITUDE AT THE END OF THE DAY

YOU WILL NEED
*a gold item, a glass container or jar,
3 cloves, a bay leaf*

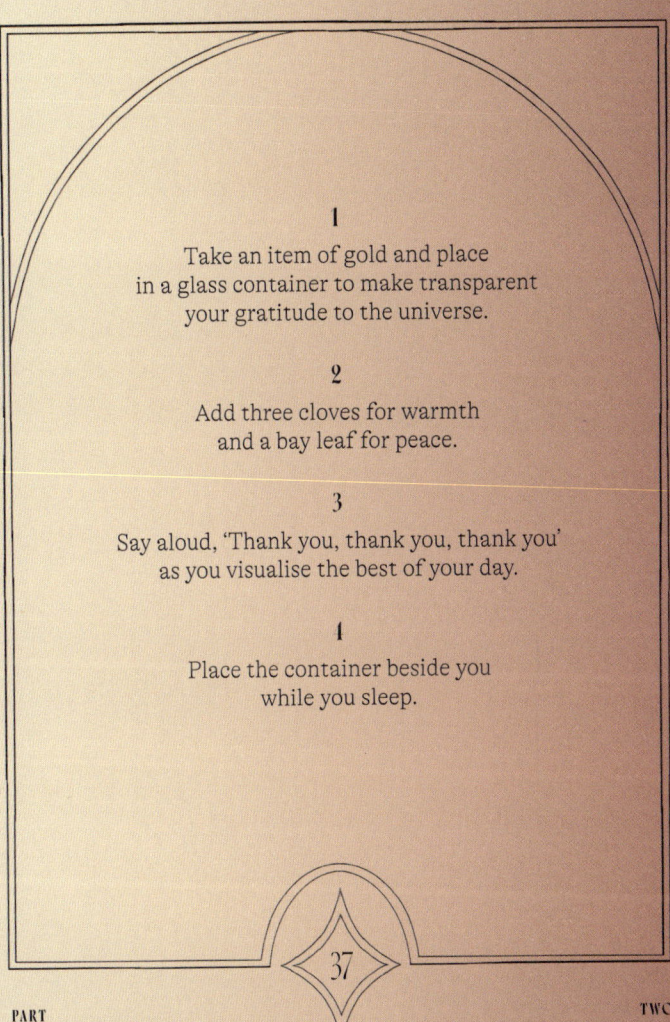

1

Take an item of gold and place
in a glass container to make transparent
your gratitude to the universe.

2

Add three cloves for warmth
and a bay leaf for peace.

3

Say aloud, 'Thank you, thank you, thank you'
as you visualise the best of your day.

4

Place the container beside you
while you sleep.

Emergency Spells for Love

Love can have its ups and downs, endings
and new beginnings, but the capacity to
love lies within us all. Draw on this when
you want to find love and when you want
to recover from love's break-up. The heart is
a resilient muscle and cannot be damaged
by loving. If you have the capacity to love,
you will always love again.

· 1 ·

TO ATTRACT SOMEONE'S ATTENTION

YOU WILL NEED
*paper, a pen, rose oil or rose petals
(fresh or dried), red thread*

1

Write down the name
of your love on paper.

2

Place a single drop of rose oil on the paper,
or fold the paper around some fresh
or dried rose petals.

3

Take a length of red thread and bind
this around the paper three times only,
tying the two ends in a single knot.

4

In a quiet voice, as you visualise their face,
say their name aloud three times.

*For greater effect, do this on a Friday, the day of the week
ruled by Venus, the goddess of love.*

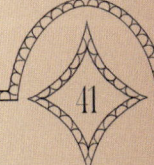

41

· 2 ·

TO RESTORE LOVE AFTER AN ARGUMENT

YOU WILL NEED

*3 bay leaves, a glass container or jar,
sugar, a sage stick, a bell*

1

Take three bay leaves and place
in a glass container.

2

Add a sprinkle of sugar to sweeten
your intention.

3

Light the sage stick and smudge
the air with the smoke.

4

Ring a bell three times to banish
the negative energy.

5

Repeat the incantation,
'Venus will restore my love' three times.

*Use sage with care if you or other family members have asthma,
and always make sure you extinguish the stick after use.*

43

TO ENHANCE
A LONGSTANDING
RELATIONSHIP

YOU WILL NEED
*paper, a red pen, rosemary oil,
green thread, red thread*

1

Write the name of your love in red pen
and encircle it with a heart shape.

2

Add a drop of rosemary oil to remind you
of why you love them.

3

Fold the paper in three and secure
with a green thread.

4

Repeat the incantation,
'Our love is strong' three times.

5

Place the tied paper in the
moonlight overnight.

45

IF YOUR SEX LIFE HAS LOST ITS OOMPH

YOU WILL NEED
a small square of red silk (or cotton),
bergamot oil, cayenne pepper

1

Give it an emergency boost by taking
a small square of red fabric, silk if possible.

2

Scent it with one drop of bergamot oil
and a sprinkle of cayenne pepper.

3

Place it in a hip pocket and focus on your
most erotic memory with your partner.

4

Silently repeat their name as an incantation
of your desire for them.

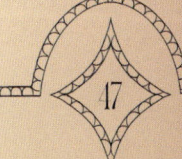

47

· 5 ·

TO HELP COPE WITH A BROKEN HEART

YOU WILL NEED
a candle, paper, a purple pen, an amethyst

1

Light a candle to illuminate the future,
in which you can trust.

2

In this light, draw a heart that's
whole and strong on paper.

3

Then draw a purple outline around
the heart and fold the paper twice.

4

Place the folded paper underneath
an amethyst overnight.

5

As you do so, repeat the incantation,
'My heart is strong, I will love again' three times.

49

Emergency Spells for Health

Your own health is your responsibility
and part of caring for yourself.
Sometimes this requires more focus
and some emergency first-aid.
In addition, you can cast spells for
those you love to help support them
in ill-health or adversity.

51

· 1 ·

TO HASTEN RECOVERY AFTER AN ILLNESS THAT HAS LEFT YOU FEELING WEAK AND FATIGUED

YOU WILL NEED

3 bay leaves, a glass container or jar, red cloth, salt

1

Take three bay leaves and
crush them in your hand.

2

Place these in a glass container
on top of a piece of red cloth,
in direct sunlight.

3

Add a pinch of salt
to strengthen the energy.

4

Say aloud three times, 'My strength
returns with each breath', as you imagine
strength returning to your body.

*If you want to support someone else's convalescence,
visualise that person as you cast this spell. This spell is enhanced
when cast on a Sunday or Tuesday.*

53

· 2 ·

TO RELIEVE AN INCIPIENT HEADACHE

YOU WILL NEED
*lemon-balm leaves (fresh or dried), chamomile heads,
(fresh or dried), a cup, honey or sugar*

1

Take a couple of lemon-balm
leaves and camomile heads.

2

Shred and place into a cup and cover
with just-boiled water to infuse.

3

Add a teaspoon of honey or sugar
and leave for five minutes.

4

Strain and dilute with a pint of cold water.

5

Sip slowly while breathing deeply
the herbal aromas.

6

Face west and click your fingers several
times to re-ground your energy.

· 3 ·

TO SOOTHE MENSTRUAL CRAMPS

YOU WILL NEED:
a flannel (washcloth), lavender oil,
rose petals (fresh or dried)

1

Make a poultice by soaking a flannel
in hot water to which you've added three
drops of lavender oil and rose petals.

2

Wring out the flannel and place on the lower
abdomen while lying flat, with knees bent and
feet flat on the floor.

3

Breathe deeply into the belly, relax and exhale;
avoid tightening against the cramps.

4

On each exhalation, repeat the incantation
'Release' to the cervical opening.

5

Snack on something magnesium-rich such
as dark chocolate, avocado or almonds.

· 4 ·

TO COMBAT NAUSEA

YOU WILL NEED

*2 inch piece of ginger-grated, a small bowl, a mug,
1 teaspoon honey or sugar, cayenne pepper, clear quartz*

1

Place your grated ginger in a small bowl
and cover with boiling water to infuse.

2

After five minutes, add a teaspoon of honey
or sugar and a pinch of cayenne pepper, then strain
into the mug and top with more water.

3

Hold a clear quartz in your left hand
as you sip slowly.

4

Gently rub your belly and breathe deeply
in through your nose and out through
your mouth.

5

Repeat the incantation,
'Banish sickness' three times.

*Ginger is your friend to combat nausea,
but you can also use fresh mint.*

59

TO RESTORE SLEEP

YOU WILL NEED
dried lavender, blue candle, pencil, paper, eraser, rose quartz

1

Rub some dried lavender between
your hands to release the scent.

2

Face north to ground your energy
and light a blue candle.

3

By the light of this candle, write down
any concerns from the day in pencil.

4

Focus on these as you gently erase them,
repeating the word 'Gone' as you do so.

5

Fold the now-blank paper in three and lay
it under a rose quartz crystal overnight.

Carry out this spell an hour before going to bed.

61

Emergency Spells for Confidence

Even the most confident person can have moments of self-doubt. An emergency spell can be useful to help you focus or refocus on your own self-worth and allow you to take that confidence into the room with you.

· 1 ·

FOR AN IMMINENT WORKPLACE EVENT

YOU WILL NEED
your birthstone

1

Take your birthstone
in your left hand.

2

Temporarily remove your shoes
and face north to ground yourself.

3

Visualise yourself within the situation,
surrounded by a green light.

4

Breathe deeply and repeat three times,
'I have the power'.

5

Keep your birthstone
in your pocket.

65

· 2 ·

FOR A JOB INTERVIEW

YOU WILL NEED
3 feathers, a rosemary sprig, red thread

1

On the morning of the interview,
make a talisman. Gather three feathers
to help you fly.

2

Add a sprig of rosemary to focus your mind.

3

Bind them together with a red thread
and place in your pocket.

4

As you do so, say three times, 'I have got this'.

5

Keeping this talisman close will strengthen
your presence in the interview.

· 3 ·

FOR A SOCIAL EVENT

YOU WILL NEED

a glass container or jar, dried nettle leaves,
ylang-ylang oil, your birthstone

1

Prior to the event, take a glass container
to make transparent your intent.

2

Place some dried nettle leaves inside
with a few drops of ylang-ylang oil.

3

Shake these together to infuse with your energy
and place the jar beside your birthstone.

4

Repeat the incantation,
'I bring my best self to this event' three times.

69

FOR A PRESENTATION THAT REQUIRES YOU TO RELY ON YOUR VOICE

YOU WILL NEED
neroli oil, blue cloth or scarf, clear quartz

1

Place a couple of drops of neroli oil
on a blue cloth or scarf.

2

Wrap this loosely around your throat.

3

Hold a piece of clear quartz in your
left hand as you hum so that you can
feel the vibrations.

4

Turn around on the spot three times.

5

Repeat your opening statement aloud
so that your voice feels familiar to you.

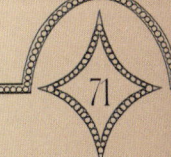

71

· 5 ·

FOR A FIRST DATE

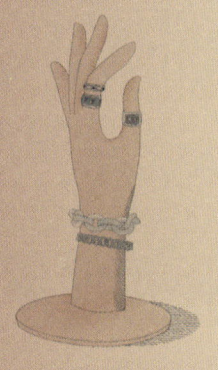

YOU WILL NEED:
poppy seeds (or any other seeds),
a glass jar, silver jewellery

1

Take a handful of seeds –
poppy seeds are preferable, but any will do –
and place in a glass jar.

2

Add a piece of silver jewellery you love.

3

Hold the jar near your heart and visualise
the person you're going to meet.

4

Smile at them in your mind's eye while
you say their name.

5

Leave the jar near your bed until you return.

73

Emergency Spells for Creativity

Coming up with ideas, fixing problems and making interesting connections are all part of creativity, and often part of how we work and live. But sometimes we can feel really uninspired and stuck. On those days, try these emergency spells to help shift and recharge your creative energy.

· 1 ·

TO SPARK INSPIRATION

YOU WILL NEED
*a head of nettle (fresh or dried), a glass jar,
rainwater (tap water will do), 1 teaspoon salt,
yellow pen or crayon, paper*

1

Take the head of a nettle.

2

Place in a glass jar with
an inch of rainwater.

3

Add a teaspoon of salt and leave
in sunlight or the light of a lamp.

4

With a yellow pen (or crayon)
write down three things that inspire you.

5

Fold the paper three times
and place in the jar.

6

Leave for 24 hours and see what
comes to mind.

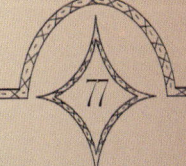

77

TO SOLVE
A PROBLEM

YOU WILL NEED
a key, white paper, cayenne pepper, a pen,
a glass container or jar

1

Take a key and lay it
on a piece of white paper.

2

Sprinkle with cayenne pepper so that
an outline remains when you remove the key.

3

Write down the problem you wish
to solve across the outline of the key.

4

Fold the paper three times and place in
a glass container in a south-facing light.

· 3 ·

TO MAKE INTERESTING CONNECTIONS

YOU WILL NEED
red thread, yellow thread, green thread,
sugar, paper, ceramic container

1

Take a red, yellow and green piece
of thread and twist together.

2

Sprinkle some sugar
on a piece of paper.

3

Fold three times and wrap the threads
around this three times also.

4

Hold in your left hand and speak the word
'Connect' out loud seven times.

5

Place in a ceramic container
and leave for 24 hours.

81

FOR THOSE HUMDRUM DAYS WHEN CURIOSITY IS HARD TO COME BY

YOU WILL NEED
*a clear quartz, yellow cloth, 3 cloves,
a glass jar, a bell*

1

Take a piece of clear quartz.

2

Wrap in a piece of yellow cloth
along with three cloves.

3

Place in a glass jar and repeat,
'Curiouser and curiouser' three times.

4

Ring a bell three times.

5

Follow up the first three thoughts that
come to mind and see where they take you.

· 5 ·

FOR INCREASED FOCUS

YOU WILL NEED
clear quartz, paper, a blue pen

1

Take a piece of clear quartz.

2

Wrap in a piece of paper on which you've
written the word 'Focus' in a blue pen.

3

With your left hand, hold this at
abdominal level and breathe deeply.

4

With eyes closed,
repeat 'I am focused' three times.

5

Place the quartz nearby as a reminder.

Emergency Spells for Protection

These spells can be incredibly useful in an emergency, particularly in the wider world like school, college or the workplace. They will help protect you against the negative energies of other people, strengthening you without damaging those around you.

· 1 ·

TO GUARD AGAINST GENERAL TOXIC ENERGY

YOU WILL NEED

*a head of fresh garlic, salt, a glass jar,
a silk bag or square (optional)*

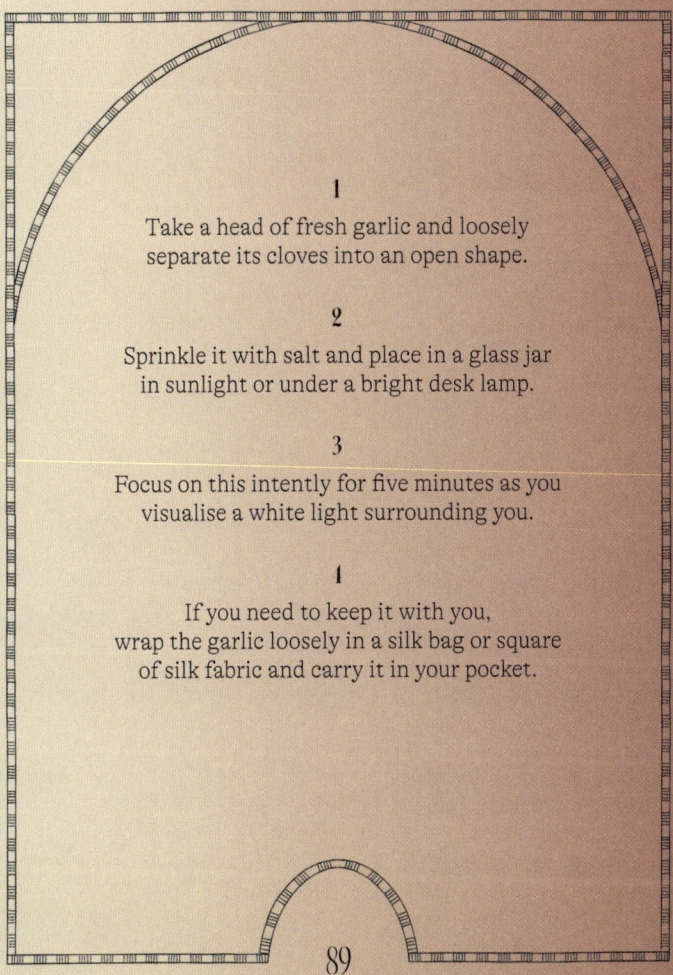

1

Take a head of fresh garlic and loosely
separate its cloves into an open shape.

2

Sprinkle it with salt and place in a glass jar
in sunlight or under a bright desk lamp.

3

Focus on this intently for five minutes as you
visualise a white light surrounding you.

4

If you need to keep it with you,
wrap the garlic loosely in a silk bag or square
of silk fabric and carry it in your pocket.

· 2 ·

TO GUARD
AGAINST NEGATIVE
PEOPLE

YOU WILL NEED
3 red threads

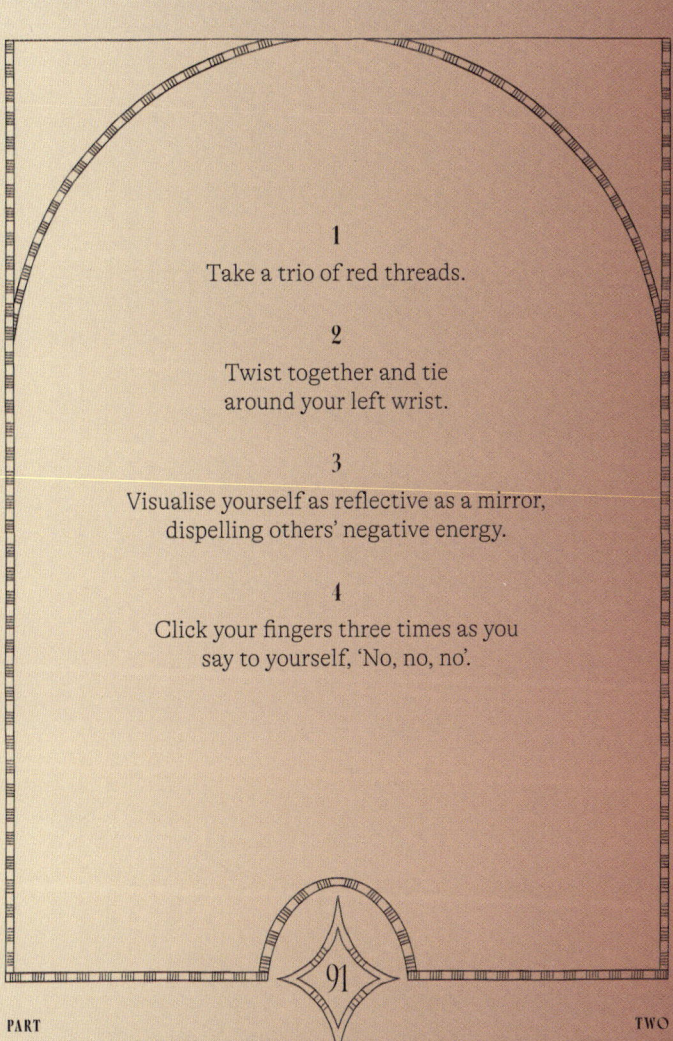

1

Take a trio of red threads.

2

Twist together and tie
around your left wrist.

3

Visualise yourself as reflective as a mirror,
dispelling others' negative energy.

4

Click your fingers three times as you
say to yourself, 'No, no, no'.

91

· 3 ·

PROTECTION AGAINST PSYCHIC LOWS

YOU WILL NEED
a sage bundle, a bell

1

Open your windows to enable
any negative energy to leave.

2

Light the end of a smudge stick,
then blow it out so it smokes. Smudge around
doorways, to prevent negative energy entering.

2

Reinforce by ringing
a small bell to dispel it further.

3

As you ring the bell, visualise
a white light around you.

4

Let the word 'protect' resonate in your mind.

*Use sage with care if you or other family members have asthma,
and always make sure you extinguish the stick after use.*

93

· 4 ·

TO BANISH THE
ENVY OF OTHERS

YOU WILL NEED:

*a green pen or crayon, paper, sugar or honey,
a metal bowl*

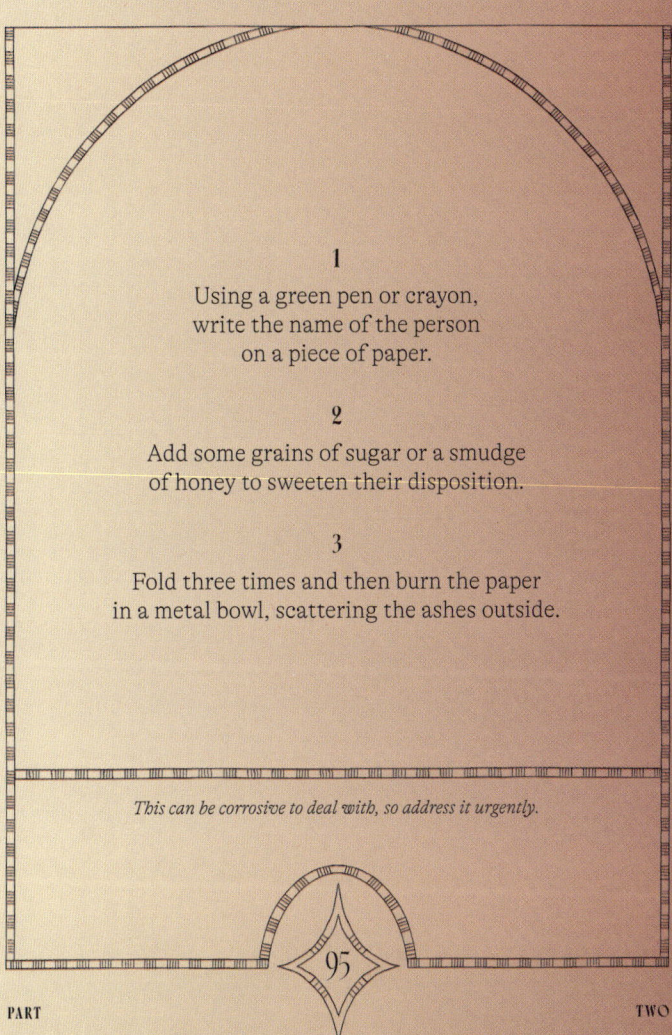

1

Using a green pen or crayon,
write the name of the person
on a piece of paper.

2

Add some grains of sugar or a smudge
of honey to sweeten their disposition.

3

Fold three times and then burn the paper
in a metal bowl, scattering the ashes outside.

This can be corrosive to deal with, so address it urgently.

· 5 ·

TO CREATE CALMING VIBES

YOU WILL NEED:
*rain water (tap water will do), a glass jar,
chamomile heads (fresh or dried), lemon balm
leaves (fresh or dried), bergamot oil*

1

Take an inch
of rainwater in a glass jar.

2

Infuse with chamomile heads,
lemon balm leaves and three drops of bergamot oil.

3

Place in a sunlit, west-facing aspect.

4

As you do so, repeat the word
'Calm' three times to yourself, sealing the spell.

*This will help you and those around you,
and can be useful in the workplace.*

97

Emergency Spells for Your Home

Your home should always be your sanctuary, your safe place, where you can shut the door on the troubles of the world. But it doesn't always feel like that, and it can take a while for a living space to feel like 'home'. Use these emergency spells when you need to focus energy in your home.

TO BLESS
YOUR NEW HOME

YOU WILL NEED
*a white candle, yellow cloth, lemon balm leaves
(fresh or dried), salt, your birthstone,
a glass container or jar*

1

Open your windows.

2

Light a white candle and place
in an east-facing aspect of your room.

3

Take a yellow cloth and wrap it around
some lemon balm leaves, a sprinkle of salt
and your birthstone.

4

Place this in a glass container
next to your candle.

5

Repeat the incantation,
'Bless my home' as you do so.

101

2

TO BANISH PAST OCCUPANTS' VIBES

YOU WILL NEED
a sage bundle

1

Light a bundle of sage and blow out
the flame so that it creates smoke.

2

Waft this in all four corners of a room.

3

Repeat, 'Old energy out, new energy in'
seven times as you do so.

4

Allow new energy to blow in.

*Use sage with care if you or other family members have asthma,
and always make sure you extinguish the stick after use.*

$\cdot\ 3\ \cdot$

TO ENHANCE POSITIVE ENERGY

YOU WILL NEED
green thread, a white candle, salt

1

Tie and knot a green thread around
a white candle, an inch from its top.

2

Light the candle and place it safely
in the middle of the room.

3

Sprinkle a pinch of salt into the flames.

4

As you do so, repeat the words,
'Bring energy to my home' seven times
while you gently tap your sternum.

5

Leave the candle to burn down to the level
of the thread before extinguishing it.

105

TO FOSTER SAFE VIBES WHEN THE WORLD FEELS UNCERTAIN

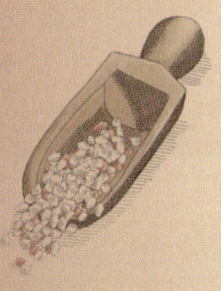

YOU WILL NEED
salt, rosemary (fresh or dried), a bell

1

Visualise a white light and an ancestor
you trusted extending their hand to you.

2

Take a pinch of salt mixed with rosemary
in your left hand to heighten your focus.

3

With your right hand, shake a bell
to banish negative energy.

4

Breathe deeply and repeat,
'I am safe' three times.

· 5 ·

TO CREATE A FEELING OF SANCTUARY

YOU WILL NEED
dried lavender

1

Keep a bowl of dried lavender
near your front door.

2

On entering your home, stir the bowl's
contents with your fingers.

3

Touch your forehead with your
scented fingers.

4

Remove your shoes to make
direct contact with the floor.

5

Repeat three times, 'I am home'.

109

Acknowledgements

First and foremost, thanks are due to
my inspirational and creative publisher
Kate Pollard, who is always willing to go
the extra mile to produce books of
substance and beauty. And to the
illustrator, Lucy Pollard, and design team
at Evi O. Studio for creating such
a gorgeous series of books.

Thanks are also due to my teachers, past
and present, who inspired me on my
journey as an esoteric practitioner,
enabling me to develop my own skills and
talents. And to my Romany grandmother
who provided insights into a world beyond
our immediate reality, and access to it.

Finally, to my family on this journey we call
life, thank you for your support and love.

About the Author

Gaia Elliot is a green witch based in London. She loves tending to her garden and being surrounded by the abundance of nature, which feeds into her spell-casting and magic-making. Gaia believes that anyone can harness their inner power by tapping into their intuition. She has a strong interest in tarot, the power of the moon and psychology. Gaia's spiritual journey started when she was a young woman, and she loves nothing more than helping other people to start or continue their own. She is the author of *The Book of Answers* and *The Pocket Mystic: Manifesting*, also published by Hardie Grant.

Published in 2024 by Hardie Grant Books (London)

Hardie Grant Books (London)
5th & 6th Floors
52–54 Southwark Street
London SE1 1UN
hardiegrantbooks.com

All rights reserved. No part of this publication may be reproduced,
stored in a retrieval system or transmitted in any form by any
means, electronic, mechanical, photocopying, recording or
otherwise, without the prior written permission of the publishers
and copyright holders.

The moral rights of the author have been asserted.

Copyright text © Gaia Elliot
Copyright illustrations © Lucy Pollard

British Library Cataloguing-in-Publication Data.
A catalogue record for this book is available from
the British Library.

Pocket Mystic: Emergency Spells
ISBN: 978-1-78488-967-8
10 9 8 7 6 5 4 3 2 1

Publishing Director: Kate Pollard
Copy Editor: Hannah Boursnell
Proofreader: Gill Hutchison
Design: Evi O. Studio
Illustrator: Lucy Pollard
Production Controller: Martina Georgieva
Colour reproduction by p2d

Printed in China by
RR Donnelley Asia Printing Solution Limited

MIX
Paper | Supporting
responsible forestry
FSC
www.fsc.org
FSC® C018179

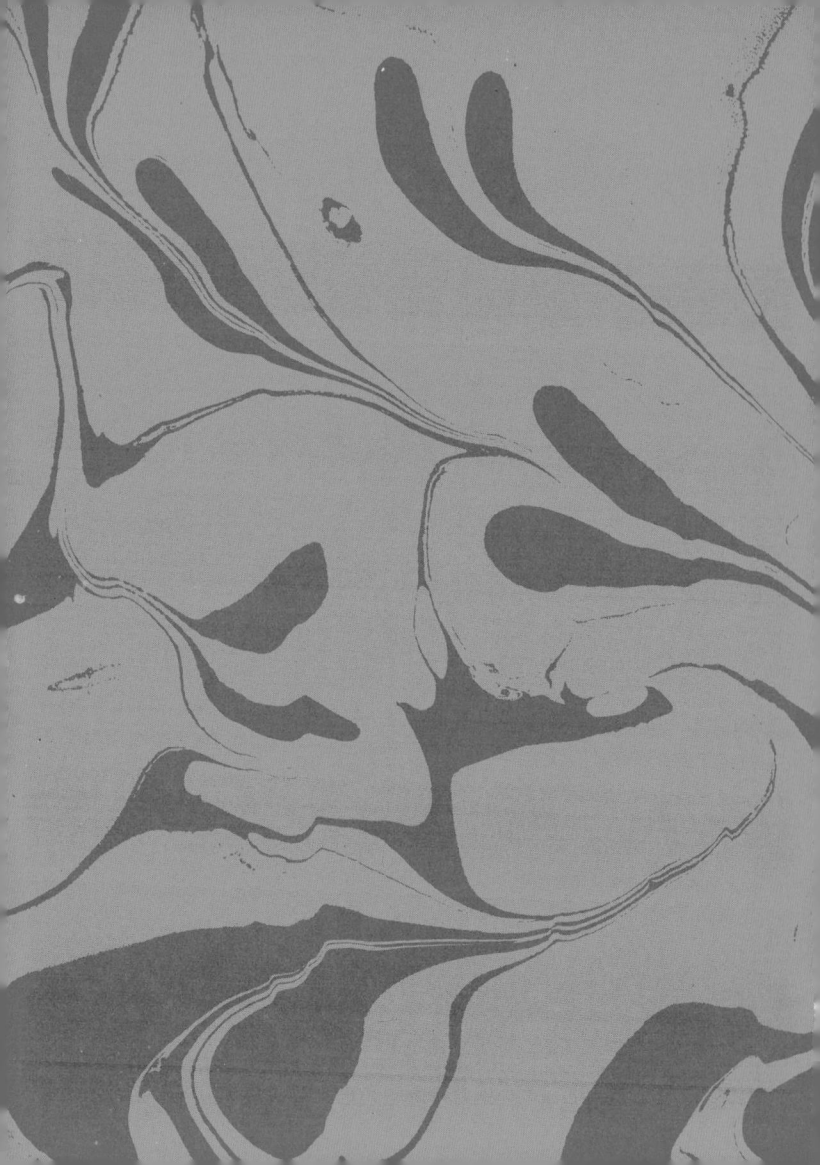